AF225255

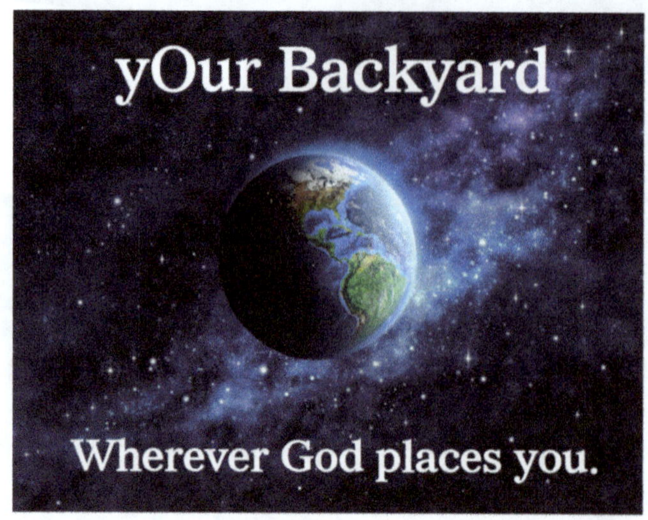

Welcome to yOur Backyard

yOur Backyard Magazine, part of yourbackyard.us; a bi-monthly online and print "on demand" publication, encourages writers, actors, artists, musicians, photographers, gardeners, crafters, and youth [of all ages]. We also offer contests with the potential to be included in forthcoming issues of yOur Backyard Magazine and yOur Backyard books.

For each bi-monthly issue, we consider:

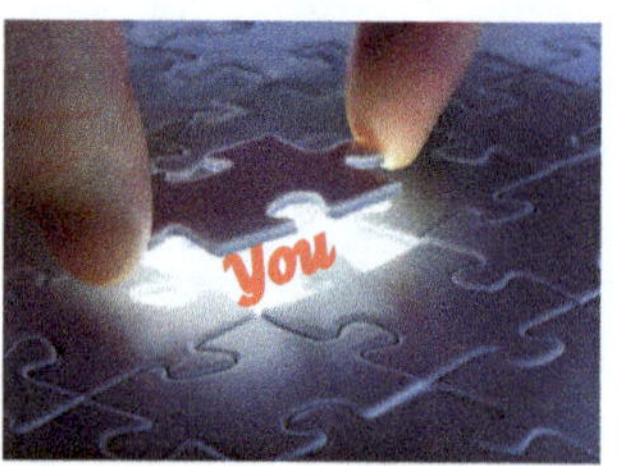

- Personal inspirational stories
- Poems
- Artwork
- Songs
- Photographs
- Biblical facts and/or applications

yOur Backyard, based on Luke 14:23, appreciates prayer.

**And the lord said unto the servant,
Go out into the highways and hedges,
and compel them to come in,
that my house may be filled.**

shELAH, editor and publisher
yOur Backyard Magazine

We look forward to hearing from you...

In this Issue...

Mary Had a Baby Boy

LouEllen Hoffman

Mary had a baby Boy,
born in Bethlehem so small...
Yet that little Baby Boy
held the whole wide world in His hands.
He made us... He loved us.
He came to save the world He loved.
He came to save us all.

That little Baby Mary held so dear; so close to her heart
Held the universe together; He kept it from falling apart.
That little Baby—Jesus Christ my Lord.
Waits on high till one day, as He promised,
He will call us to His side.

Mary's little Baby proclaimed by that bright star
Drew shepherds running to Him and wise men from afar.
Mary's little Baby became the sacrificial Lamb
He hung on the cross for us,
even though He was—the great "I AM."
He died for us but rose again, and now He waits above
Praying for and helping us, keeping us in His love.

My friend, do you know my Jesus?
Oh friend, I pray that you do.
He loves us. He died for us.
He loves me... He loves you.
He did not stay in the manger.
He did not stay on that tree.
He left that tomb and then went home
to build a place for you...for me.

Thank God for our wonderful Savior,
Thank God for His mercy and love.
Thank God for the day
He was born in that manger.
Thank God though He died, He rose again.
Today, because He lives
We who believe in Him have eternal life.
Because Mary had a baby Boy.
Jesus...

"I've never done a painting so quickly...," **Carla Taylor**, the artist for the cover of this issue of y*Our Backyard*, said. She and Roger, married for 25 years, have four children together.

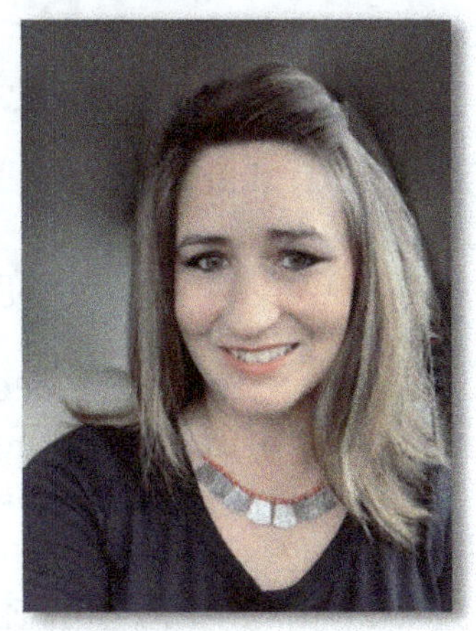

"I typically paint from pictures I take or from something visual," Carla explained. "It's hard for me to just paint something from my mind. But God told me to do a little church with the door open and the light pouring out.

"The light of Jesus, 'The Light of the world,' shines brightly for us to see.

"As the star helped guide the wise men so many years ago to find Jesus, I positioned it in the painting to represent the light guiding us to where Jesus waits for us. Thus, I entitled this painting 'His door is always open.'

"His door is not only 'always open for us,' He makes the entrance easy. We just have to take the step to accept His invitation."

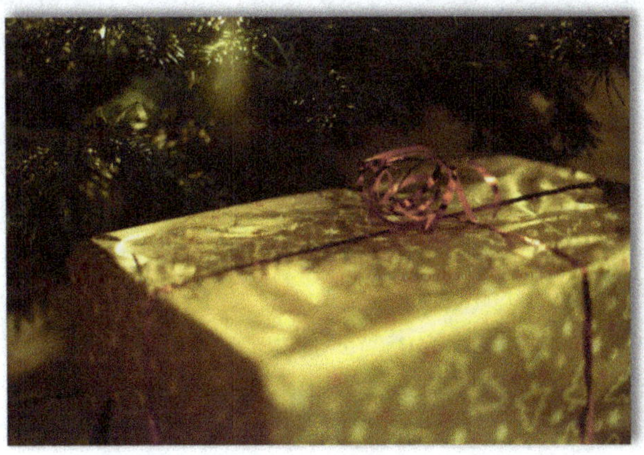

Image by karosieben from Pixabay

**For unto you is born this day in the city of David
a Saviour, which is Christ the Lord.
And this shall be a sign unto you;
Ye shall find the babe wrapped in swaddling clothes,
lying in a manger.**
~ Luke 2:12 – 13

I Believe in Angels

"I believe in angels…"

Billy Graham wrote in his book, *Angels: Ringing Assurance that We Are Not Alone:*

I do not believe in angels because I have ever seen one – because I haven't.

I believe in angels because the Bible says there are angels; and I believe the Bible to be the true word of God.

I also believe in angels because I have sensed their presence in my life on special occasions.

A 2016 Gallup poll reported that 72% of Americans believe in angels; 12% are not sure, and that 16% do not believe in angels.

Fox News reported that though far from universal, surveys show a widespread belief in angels in some parts of the world.

While Italians and Croatians are on par with Americans, for instance, no more than a third of Danes believe in angels—somewhere between 25 and 33 percent, according to the European Values Study. The English are similarly low; just 36 percent believe in angels, according to Gallup.

These numbers seem to roughly correlate to belief in God.

"Dr." Luke records one of my favorite reports of angels:

Then she [Mary] gave birth to her firstborn Son [Jesus], and she wrapped Him snugly in cloth and laid Him in a feeding trough—because there was no room for them at the lodging place.

In the same region, shepherds were staying out in the fields and keeping watch at night over their flock. Then an angel of the Lord stood before them, and the glory of the Lord shone around them, and they were terrified. But the angel said to them, "Don't be afraid, for look, I proclaim to you good news of great joy that will be for all the people: Today a Savior, who is Messiah the Lord, was born for you in the city of David. This will be the sign for you: You will find a baby wrapped snugly in cloth and lying in a feeding trough" (Luke 2: 7 – 13, HCSB).

Sue Bohlin warns that in addition to good angels such as the ones that appeared to the shepherds, bad angels also exist. Unholy angels, approximately one third of original angels created as holy angels; like Satan, rebelled against God. The Bible warns these demons (unholy angels) serve Satan and that Satan sometimes times masquerades as an angel of light (2 Corinthians. 11:14).

Billy Graham stresses we do not have to fear Satan or his angels; that the message the angels proclaimed years ago to the shepherds proves true today.

The message of peace, protection, and power the angels shared that first Christmas applies today. Instead of letting fear steal our peace and joy... Instead of worrying about what might happen tomorrow... We can experience peace during this and every season in our lives as we not only trust the Bible to be the true word of God, but also Jesus, the One Who left the privileges of Heaven for a season. We can trust the One Who grew from a Baby born in in a feeding trough; Who in time died on the cross to give us eternal life; Who gave us the gift of peace.

We can enjoy the gift Jesus left us; recorded in John 14: 27: "Peace I leave with you. My peace I give to you. I do not give to you as the world gives. Your heart must not be troubled or fearful." That peace empowers us; whether we recognize the presence of an angel or not, to live without fear; to live with peace, love, hope and faith.

Like Billy Graham, when we know the gift of God, Jesus, the One Heaven's holy angels came to proclaim; we will likely say, "I believe in angels." When we study God's Word, we can say we believe that angels exist "because the Bible says there are angels."

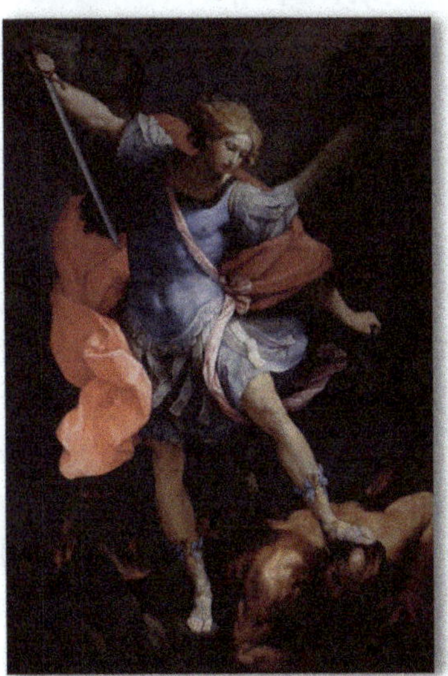

Guido Reni: Michael Defeats Satan
Public Domain

For he shall give his angels charge over thee,
to keep thee in all thy ways.
~ Psalm 91:11

Angels: Not Like Hollywood Shows

"I do not believe in angels," Kenneth, a seminary student during the 60's, said.

At the time, Kenneth considered angels as relics of an outdated, religious belief system. When asked to sing a song with words similar to "Angels we have heard on high," Kenneth and another student refused to sing the song because it related to angels.

"We were wrong," Kenneth later concluded. "Angels do exist."

During Christmas, more than other times of the year, thoughts of angels as well as recognition of their existence appear more pronounced. The word angel occurs 203 times in 194 verses in the King James Version (KJV) of the Holy Bible while the word "angels" occurs 94 times in 92 verses. One meaning of "angel" indicates an angel of the Lord to be a messenger or representative of God.

The word "angel," which evolves from the Greek word angelos, means "messenger." The Holy Bible includes almost 300 accounts of angels carrying out some kind of service for God. Angels may also sometimes "minister" to people. In the book, *Angels Among Us: Separating Fact from Fiction,* Ron Rhodes explains:

- [A]ngelic ministry may involve protection (Psalm 91:11),
- guidance (Genesis 19:16-17),
- encouragement (Judges 6:12),
- deliverance (Acts 2:7),
- supply (Psalm 105:40),
- enlightenment (Matthew 2:19 – 20), and
- empowerment (Luke 22:43)...

Some angels render service directly to God and Christ. Other angels bring judgment against unbelievers,,, [A]ngels are involved in carrying out the sovereign bidding of God..

Contrary to the "Hollywoodization" of angels, an angel does not get its wings every time a bell rings. In filming the movie "A Wonderful life," and other fabricated stories portraying angels—Hollywood lied.

When angels visited, humans often feared the powerful, magnificent beings. II Kings 19:35 reports that during just one night, a single angel destroyed an army of 185,000 Assyrian soldiers.

We are not only to believe angels exist, we who believe in and trust Jesus Christ do not have to fear them. After all, angels first proclaimed the good news; that God so loves us that He gave His only begotten Son...

Remember the Time...
Bill McDonald

Remember the time...?

Although some memories may be painful, they comprise part of the journey in healing after the death of a loved one. Remembering things that happened in the past helps one get to the place in time where they can step forward and begin to smile again. Those who have lost a loved one will either merely go through or grow during the grieving process. Whether a person goes or grows during this time will be centered around decisions he makes.

Living through the shadow of death does not have to be overwhelming nor does it have to be a time of complete darkness. Grief reflects the high price of loving someone, yet it also confirms the fact that a person has been loved. When remembering a loved one, it is good to remember the places you shared; the love you gave to each other. Remember the spirit of the one who walked with you. That bond can never be broken. Appreciate the time you had with your loved one as well as the time you have with those who are still an active part of your life. From what my dad said and the way he lived, I have learned some things that help ensure we make positive memories with those we love.

These include:
➢ Cleaning up relationships.
➢ Arguing less.
➢ Forgiving often.
➢ Seeking forgiveness always.

I have also learned that at times as we live through life's challenges, we need to be comforted and understood. We also need to give comfort and make a point to try to understand others. In doing so, we will see happiness and receive what we need. Our family experienced a particularly challenging time when we did not realize we needed to be comforted and understood after Ken, my older brother, died at the age of 16. For three years following Ken's death, I as well as Mom, Dad, and Bobby, my younger brother, tried individually to hide our pain.

When the Holidays Aren't Happy

Bill McDonald

The holidays may be billed as the happiest days of the year; however, when grief comes—they can be downright miserable. For those going through the "season to be jolly" without someone they love, the days drag by. If we could have, we might have pushed a magic button and propelled ourselves into January to just skip Thanksgiving and Christmas.

When I was 16, my younger brother died. I will never forget the difficulty of the years that followed. Christmas was the most difficult day of that first year, because he had been a miniature Santa Claus in disguise. He loved this holiday. That year we struggled through the day... all smiles acting as if we were OK. Inside each member of my family was in shambles. Only after a couple of holiday seasons did we get to the place where we could mention his name and reminisce about him on Christmas Day.

It took a year or two, but we finally learned that the sound of his name was just the medicine we needed to get through the tough days. The first mention of his name would often bring tears, but soon the joy of sharing stories filled with "do you remember when he..." would follow. I remember thinking how I needed to learn from all the mistakes we made following my brother's death to avoid making them when death visited our family again.

When my dad died, my resolution about learning was put to the test.

My favorite holiday with my dad was Thanksgiving. The year he died I knew I would miss him most that day. The only thing I dreaded more than Thanksgiving Day without dad was not spending Thanksgiving Day with those in my family who remained. I knew the gathering would be initially painful, especially when we gathered around the table for the blessing he always led. I also knew my mom would not have the emotional energy to have all of us out to her house, so we had to make some changes. My sweet wife cooked the meal and we all gathered together at our home. The prayer and the moments following were filled with tears, but after we thanked our Father for giving us such a wonderful man to head our family, we told stories about my dad all afternoon. It was wonderful.

Since those two experiences have helped shape my life, I have taken the time to jot down a few things I always try to remind myself of during the holiday season. These have become my guidelines for working through the especially difficult days of the year. I share these ideas hoping next year may be a little easier for us all.

Living Through the Holidays
Bill McDonald

When the holidays roll around, I like to keep the following thoughts in mind. They don't solve all the difficulties with the season; however, they seem to help make the most of these challenging times. Perhaps with a little creativity, these ideas can help you through the most difficult time of the year.

1. I am no different from anyone else in my situation. I dread the "season to be jolly."
2. I realize this holiday season will not be the same as those before.
3. I will find someone with whom I can share how I feel during this time of the year. I will honestly discuss with them how I feel, so the emotions of the season will not bottle up and catch me off guard.
4. I will remember that the longer I put off doing something, the harder doing it may become. I will therefore try to keep this in mind as I work my way through this new experience. I will also try to keep in mind how my actions might affect those I love.
5. I know that no matter how hard I may try, there will be times when I will not feel like having a good time. I am going to make this OK with myself, so I will not have to worry or apologize about this later.
6. There may come a time when I wish to go somewhere or do something. I will go and I will do. I will give myself permission to smile or laugh if I want to. I will also give myself permission to tell those with me when I need to leave. This will take pressure off me and others.
7. I have enough sense to know there are things I don't want to do; there are a number of things I don't want to miss. I will therefore alter the way I do the holidays this year. I will make an effort to keep in mind the reason for the season and change what I need to do to be able to experience the moments I do not want to miss.
8. I will work to understand that life does go on for others even though my world has stopped. I will seek for an acceptance of their sense of joy and completeness even though I am struggling.
9. I will design a way to remember the life of my loved one. I will share what I do with someone or quietly do for myself. I will seek to bless someone else in the process.
10. I will remember that next year is next year. No changes I make are set in stone. If I want to do everything next year just like last year, so be it. Likewise, I will feel free to again alter my way of celebration if the need arises.

One Foot in Heaven

SHEILA PRESTON FITZGERALD

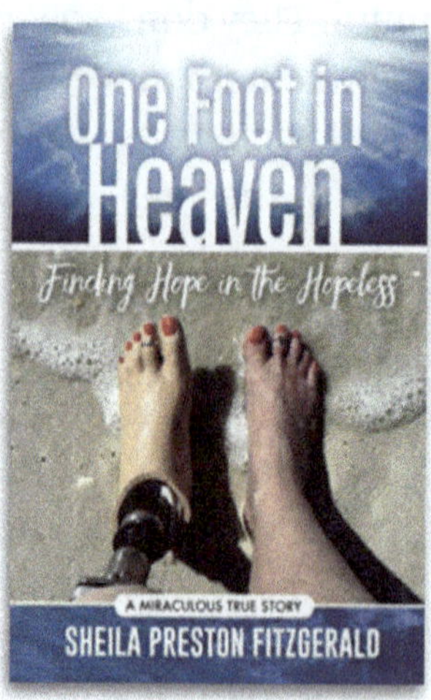

"Do you sleep with that thing?"

When a 5-year-old asks Sheila that or a similar question, she smiles and tells them, "No..." She will then tell the young one asking the question more about living her life as an amputee with a prosthesis.

When a 55-year-old male asks her that same question, however, Sheila quickly responds with a warning like, "Don't make me take this thing off and whack you with it."

Just as she does not cover up her plastic leg or foot, Shelia does not cover up her faith and trust in Jesus. As shared in last week's Checkpoints, she lost her left leg and foot due to the motorcycle accident she survived. Even though she also lost her marriage, her home, and her job, plus the ability to work as before, Sheila said she would not change all those things for what she gained. For four years, when much of the world would go to sleep at night, from the night of the accident that forever changed her life forward, Sheila entered into a relationship with Jesus... with God... with the Holy Spirit.

Often when Sheila shares her story with a group, she will start with, "How many of you know Abraham Lincoln?"

Many will respond that they do. "How?" she will ask.

Typically, the response will be, "I've read about him."

"But do you really know him?" she will continue. Sheila stresses that we don't really know someone until we have met them. I also believe that we may know about someone, but if we do not personally know them, we do not really know them.

Because of her accident, Sheila came from knowing about Jesus from what she had read; from what others said—to knowing Him.

In speaking and in writing, Sheila shares three Sheila-isms she would like others to remember:

1. Choose happy, not crappy.
2. There's no shame in being broken...what matters is what you do with the pieces.
3. Grit, grace, and gratitude.

It took Sheila a long time to realize that He chose her, and to walk on her life's journey with her. "… I'm grateful," she said. "Through my situation which has forced me to be still. God's training me. He's teaching me how to be still and to listen, and to not be so reactive." She encourages others to listen to God.

When speaking to groups, Sheila listens to and addresses questions those attending may ask. It does not matter if the one asking is a 5-year-old or a 55-year-old, Sheila regularly reminds those with hurting hearts that Jesus will help them find hope, even in times when things may seem hopeless.

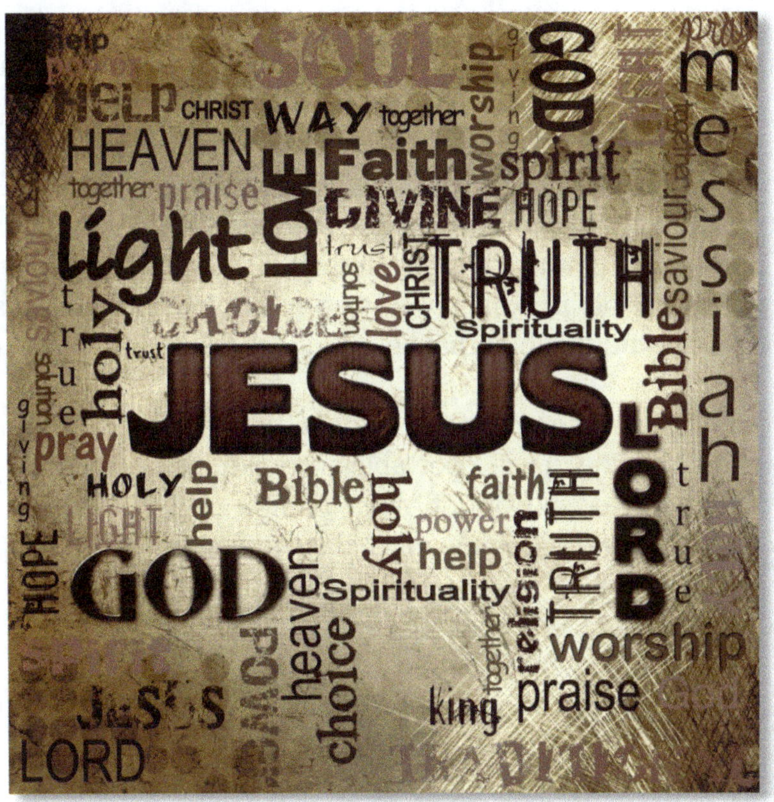

**For God sent not his Son into the world
to condemn the world;
but that the world through him
might be saved.**

~ John 3:17

Alex's Boots, a Reminder of Prayer and the Angel

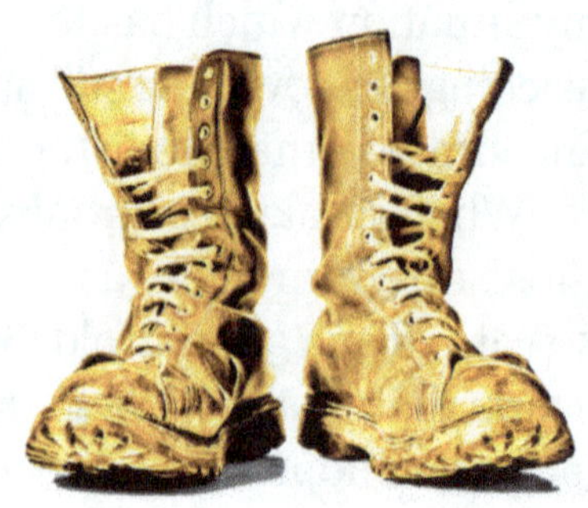

"Mama," Alex, just back from Iraq, said when he showed her the picture of his charred combat boots. "When my Humvee blew up, my boots got burned."

"Praise the Lord," Alex's mother said.

"But Mama - I could have been killed."

"You're right."

"Mama, you must have really be praying."

"I don't just pray for you each morning," Alex's mom told him. "I pray for you in the morning, at noon, and each night."

"Mama, I pray too," Alex said. "I believe we're all gonna be ok , but... remember if something happens, remember—I'll see you later in Heaven.

"My charred boots are my favorite pair of boots," Alex added.

At times, as a "country boy" from the South, Alex received verbal "jabs" from some of his Army buddies from the North. He talked about one incident reminding him that being "ribbed" is nothing to get upset about.

"Get your a...out of the way, 'Country,'" another soldier in Iraq said to Alex standing in line to use a portable potty. I'm going ahead of you," he said as he shoved in front of Alex.

"Go ahead," Alex said, knowing a place in line and a "country" jab didn't merit a fight.

"God bless you," Alex added.

"'F... you," the other soldier snapped back.

The next thing Alex knew, the blue porta-potty exploded, killing the young man who had barged in line.

"Mama," Alex later told his mother, "I prayed for him."

"I pray for you every day," Alex's mom reminded him. "I ask the Lord to please surround you with His angels.'"

"He did," Alex said. "Last month, sitting on top of my Humvee, traveling in a convoy down a road in Iraq, I noticed a man standing alone in the field on my right. As we made eye contact, I turned and pointed my 50 caliber weapon toward him. The next thing I remembered was feeling dazed and confused; picking myself up off the hard ground.

"I heard gunfire and knew I had to try to get to a safe area—fast. There was nothing to hide behind, however. At just the right time, another Humvee came around, picked up me and the other passenger who had been in the attacked Humvee. The driver transported us to a secure area.

"Later, when secure and recounting the unexpected attack, I noticed my boots were black, charred... burned, but I was not injured; not even scratched.

"Three days later, the enemy attacked another Humvee I was riding atop and destroyed it. I believe an angel kept me safe. The following Sunday, when the chaplain asked, 'Does anybody need any spiritual guidance?' I asked. Surviving two direct hits to my unit's Humvees in less than a week, I felt like God was trying to tell me something I didn't understand.

"'Don't be overwhelmed by all the negative things going on around you,' the chaplain said. 'God, was looking down and protected you.'

"Today, when I look at my blackened, charred, burned boots," Alex said, "it's one of most reassuring things that occurred during my time in Iraq.

"I prayed each day I would come back home safely; that the Good Lord would protect me; that my family and friends would do well while I was gone.

I prayed that when I returned home, I would not be missing an arm, a leg, a finger; not even a toe. I prayed I would come back physically intact; just the way I left home.

"When I returned, however, I came back with more than I left with...a stronger faith. Often when I prayed, verse 4 in Psalm 23 reassured me: 'Yea, though I walk through the valley of the shadow of death, I will fear no evil, for Thou art with me...'

"I knew God was with me, no matter what happened. Even when threatened by enemy fire and fear taunted me—I was at peace. Now, as then, I know God is in control of whatever happens.

"Anytime I need reminding of God's care... of His angels, I only have to look at the picture of my favorite boots."

**For he shall give his angels charge over thee,
to keep thee in all thy ways.**

~ Psalm 91:11

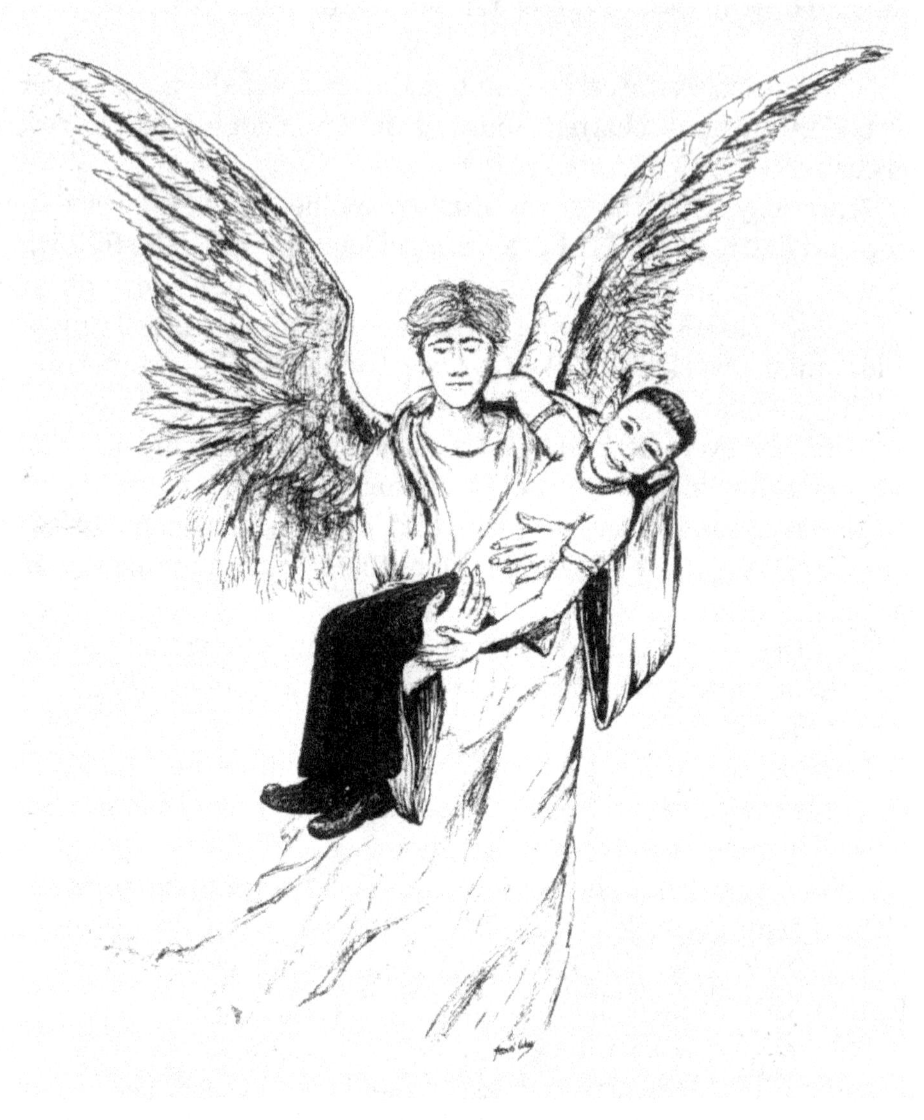

And it came to pass, that the beggar died,
and
was carried by the angels
into Abraham's bosom...
~ Luke 16:22a

When Christmas Hurts

shELAH

Wayne was one year younger than my own 13 years that Christmas I decided to hate him. Nothing that my brother had specifically said or done to me ignited my coldness toward him. Instead, it was the horrible gift he ordered for our family.

We were poor at the time. One mother with four children... Welfare poor. Being poor, however, was not the problem. Most of the time we forgot to even notice. The real problem I, as the oldest child, perceived? Wayne. My brother had no pride! After what he had done, I could never show my face at school again. Ever!
Nothing my sandy-haired, brown-eyed brother could have done would have redeemed him in my eyes. *It was all Wayne's fault, my life was ruined,* I thought.

Mother smiled as she offered me a plump juicy orange from the brimming basket of food. My sister and other brother stared amazed as they sampled some of the delicacies. *All this for us? Free?*

Not me! Though my mouth watered, my "face" refused to budge. I hated the brightly bowed bounty someone anonymously delivered and dumped at our door during the night. I hated Wayne! I hated all of them! Most of all, I hated me.

How could he? I fumed. How could my own brother turn in our family's name to be listed among the needy?

It was not the worst Christmas I remember from my childhood, but it came close. Not until years later did I finally realize that Christmas is not only a time for giving presents—but a time for receiving as well.

Wayne died five years later driving across a bridge during a thunderstorm. A 16-year-old female's car slid into the small motorcycle he rode... a few weeks before another Christmas. The memory of Wayne's concern for our family, nevertheless, still lives. So does the lesson.

The One for Whom we celebrate this holiday season said best what mortals should remember each and every Christmas. John 12 records that when Judas Iscariot criticized Mary was for her extravagant gift of pouring an expensive perfume on Jesus' feet, He made one point plain. "For ye have the poor always with you; but me ye have not always" (Matthew 26:11).

This Christmas, take time to appreciate each and every gift you receive—and the Giver. Who knows? Five years from now, you may wish you had.

Cancer Can't Steal Christmas

Leighann McCoy

I love Christmas.

I hate cancer and other icky things. Although cancer and other bad things can steal a lot of things, they can never steal Christmas.

In 2010, I was diagnosed with colon cancer. In 2012 that cancer re-appeared in my liver. I had surgery to remove the cancer (June) and underwent 6 months of chemotherapy treatment (August – January).

On July 14, 2012, one of my most difficult days, I received the news that my surgery for cancer in my liver was not 100% successful. That same day, Daddy wrote me the following intimate email. I'm sharing it in hopes that for those of you who are struggling through the holidays, you will find great comfort in the TRUTH he speaks and the message of Christmas that remains unstoppable.

Your mother told me the results of your doctor visit.

If your life shows anything, it's that God has called you. What you have done (and what you will do) is the result of His doing, ...not anything your mother and I have done. Whatever your future holds, it's all good.

But you know that. Your greatest battle going forward is not going to be trusting God,but keeping Satan's accusing, lying voice out of your head.

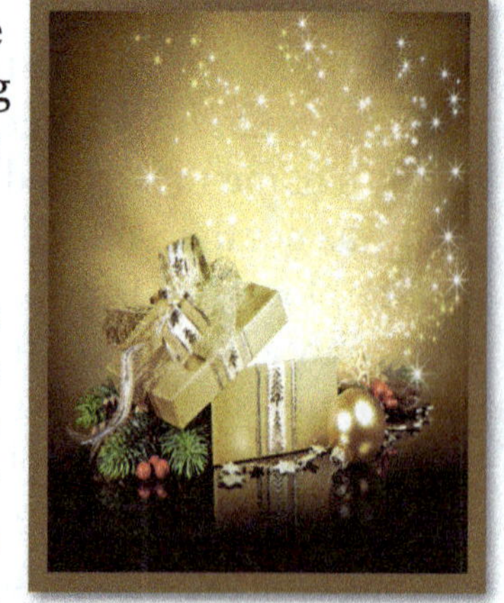

Leighann responded to her dad:

Daddy, ...Thank you for living your life in in such a way that I discovered how to find God's secret places and recognize what He considers precious there. I know beyond a shadow of a doubt had you been in Bethlehem that first Christmas, you would've found Jesus in that stable because you would've known to look for Him there.

Leighann wrote to readers:

To those suffering with cancer (or any other icky thing that causes you to struggle): "I don't like it one bit... but if we truly love Him, we will allow Him to call the shots."

And we can trust Him because He is with us. Although cancer and other icky things can steal a lot of good things—cancer can never steal Christmas.

Stille Nacht Heilige Nacht

Stille Nacht

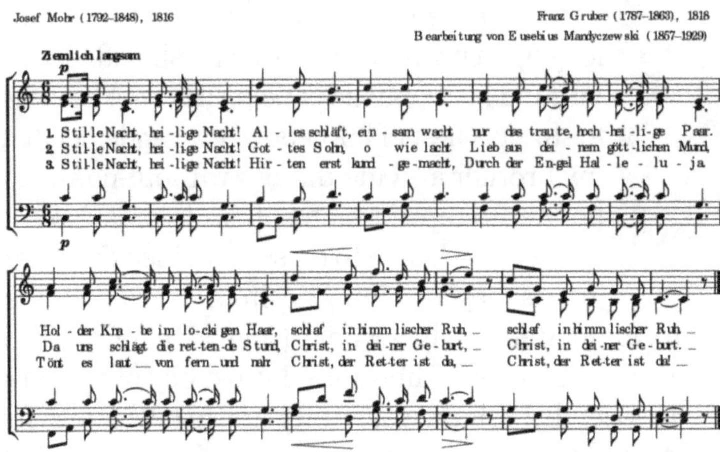

Rettinghaus - Volksliederbuch für gemischten Chor, Leipzig 1915, CC

During the fall of 1816 following the Napoleonic Wars, after mice incapacitated the church's organ, Joseph Mohr, an Austrian priest wrote the song, "Stille Nacht Heilige Nacht" in German.* On Christmas Eve in 1914, at the height of World War I, both German and British soldiers sat in mud, so close they could talk with each other.

Witnesses reported seeing candles lit in the trenches. One stated that when Germans began singing Silent Night in their language, British soldiers sang it in English. As both sides laid down their weapons, this started a spontaneous cease fire. As enemy soldiers shook hands, some wiped away tears. For a few hours, a beautiful silence echoed a "heavenly peace."

Today in 2022, lyrics of "Silent Night" translated into a minimum of 300 languages reflect God's grace through Jesus Christ; the gift of eternal life that unites Christians throughout the world. The year Mohr wrote this song, he sang it with Franz Xaver Gruber, the choir director who had written the melody. Instead of the mice-damaged organ, Mohr played the guitar to accompany them.

Silent night, holy night!
Son of God love's pure light.
Radiant beams from Thy holy face
With the dawn of redeeming grace,
Jesus Lord, at Thy birth
Jesus Lord, at Thy birth

Music—Then and Now

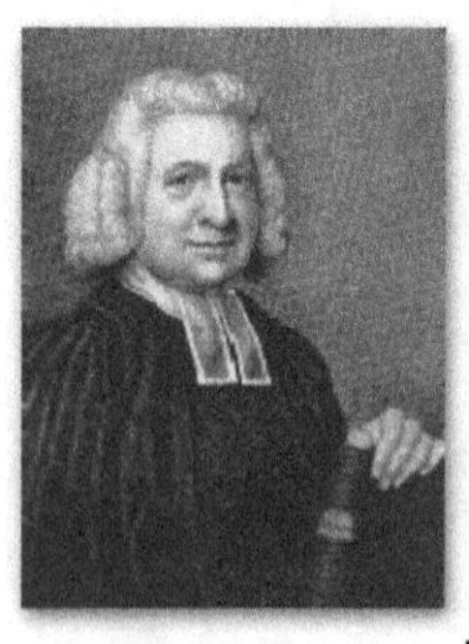

"I beg leave to mention a thought which has been long upon my mind, and which I should long ago have inserted in the public papers, had I not been unwilling to stir up a nest of hornets. Many gentlemen have done my brother and me though without naming us) the honour to reprint many of our hymns. Now they are perfectly welcome to do so, provided they print them just as they are. But I desire they would not attempt to mend them, for they are really not able. None of them is able to mend either the sense or the verse. Therefore, I must beg of them these two favours: either to let them stand just as they are, to take things for better or worse, or to add the true reading in the margin, or at the bottom of the page, that we may no longer be accountable either for the nonsense or for the doggerel of other men."

Charles Wesley, who wrote more than 6,000 hymns, Published "Hark the Herald Angels Sing" in 1739. Like most hymnists, his works were frequently altered. He wrote the above preface to one of his hymnals.

"Hark! The Herald Angels Sing"

Hark! The herald angels sing,
"Glory to the newborn King;
Peace on earth, and mercy mild,
God and sinners reconciled!"
Joyful, all ye nations rise,
Join the triumph of the skies;
With th'angelic host proclaim,
"Christ is born in Bethlehem!"

Refrain

Hark! the herald angels sing,
"Glory to the newborn King!

Christ, by highest heav'n adored;
Christ the everlasting Lord;
Late in time, behold Him come,
Offspring of a virgin's womb.

Veiled in flesh the Godhead see;
Hail th'incarnate Deity,
Pleased with us in flesh to dwell,
Jesus our Emmanuel.

Hail the heav'nly Prince of Peace!
Hail the Sun of Righteousness!
Light and life to all He brings,
Ris'n with healing in His wings.
Mild He lays His glory by,
Born that man no more may die.
Born to raise the sons of earth,
Born to give them second birth.

Refrain

Come, Desire of nations, come,
Fix in us Thy humble home...

Music — Now
A Special Tree
Jerry Arhelger

Sitting by my window on Christmas Eve,
Watching the children playing in the snow,
The lights all sparkle from the Christmas tree,
And I sat back and just enjoyed the show
Then in sad meditation,
I thought about the name [Jesus]
Was not so long ago
That little Baby King came.
There was no fame or special tree...
The Baby came; the Man remained...
to hang for me...on a special tree...
(Excerpt from "A Special Tree")

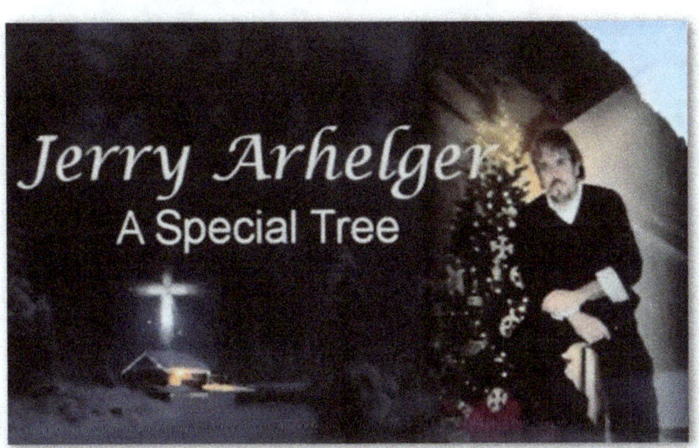

I never want to forget why Christmas time is here. I always want to remember the Special Tree—the Cross. I hope you all have a Merry Christmas and a great celebration of the Lord's birth and New Year

For those who have an empty chair around your table, I pray the song that Jill Wood and I wrote and the beautiful video Jill created will minister comfort to you until all of our friends and family gather for the greatest celebration of Joy with Our Heavenly Father and Lord Jesus. Our coming celebration was all made possible by a Tree that was Adorned by a Sacrifice of Love—Jesus.

m.facebook.com/watch/?v=1494303650597601&paipv=0&eav=AfbCV_OI6mop
gTvbhr47kmsZyzQYPzQEJoMpit1Drv2KO1RHdOd6Empp7dLdxb8xp4M&_rdr#

Why Christmas Colors of Green and Red?

Two accepted beliefs reflect the origin of traditional Christmas colors. One relates to the Christian faith, while the other recounts historical fact dating back to the 14th century.

Even though the Bible does not name the fruit Eve ate as an apple, theatrical productions of Adam and Eve in the Garden of Eden depicted it to be just that. Because the apple tree was not available year round, however, the evergreen pine emerged as a symbol of the Christian's faith in eternal life. Evergreen corresponds to everlasting.

As we celebrate the birth of Jesus Christ at Christmas, red reminds us that He shed His blood for our sins. The color red also relates to blood as it symbolizes life.

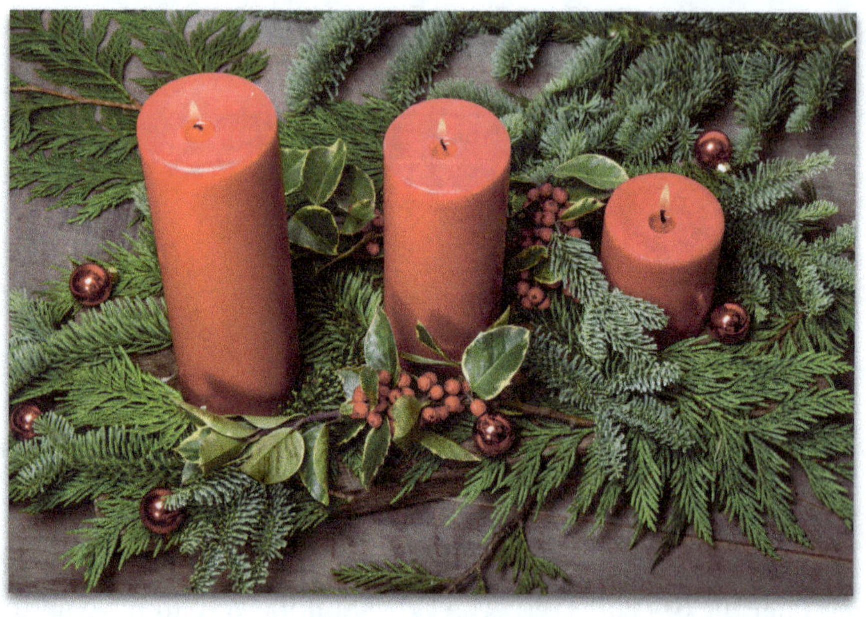

**But if we walk in the light, as he is in the light,
we have fellowship one with another,
and the blood of Jesus Christ his Son
cleanseth us from all sin.**
~ 1 John 1:7

Songs of Angels?

"I believe that angels sing."

"I do not believe that angels sing."

"I do not know if angels sing."

Some argue that numerous verses in the Holy Bible proclaim that angels sing while others cite these same verses to support their view that only humans can sing. These verses include:

† Job 38:7

† Luke 2:13-14

† Revelation 5:11-12

I agree with those who say that only those "born again" can sing about God's amazing grace. Whether angels can sing other songs, however, even though I have to say, "I do not yet know"—I like to say, as the song, "Hark, the Herald Angels Sing" proclaims—"I believe that angels sing."

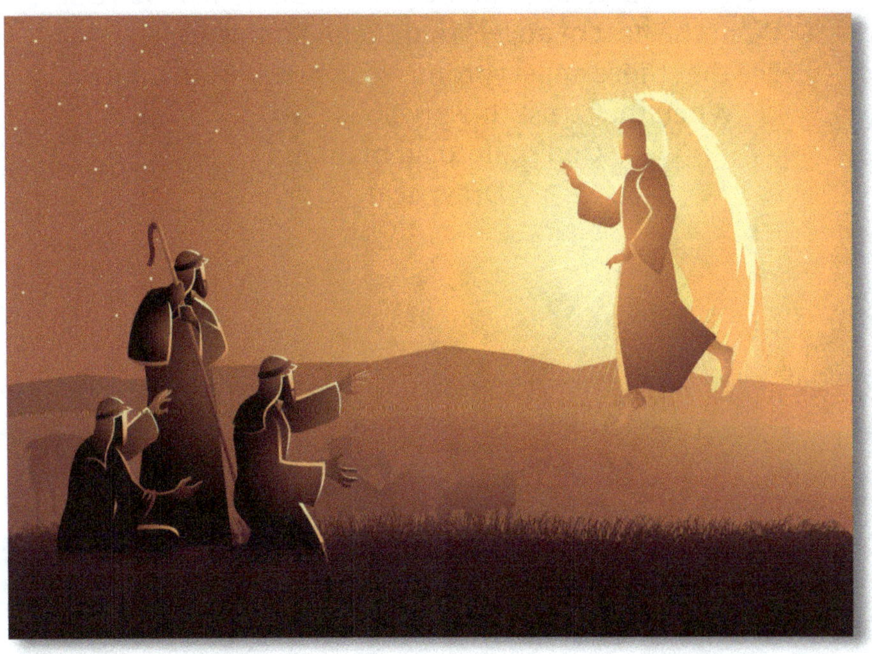

**And suddenly there was with the angel
a multitude of the heavenly host praising God,
and saying, Glory to God in the highest,
and on earth peace, good will toward men.**

~ Luke 2: 13-14

Draw Near

LouEllen Hoffman

He came as a newborn Baby, in Bethlehem born,
With angels watching over, keeping Him from harm.
Heavenly Hosts sang of His glory, telling all mankind
That God sent His Son Jesus,
The promised Savior, the Hope throughout all time.

Draw near. Draw near.
To the Son of God now here...
Draw near.
Listen... His praises we will hear.
To Jesus, our mighty Savior—draw near.

Shepherds came from the field, wanting to believe
What the host of angels told them, hoping to receive
Peace that those angels promised, a blessing all may find
When they trust this precious Baby... Jesus—
God's gift to all mankind.
Draw near.

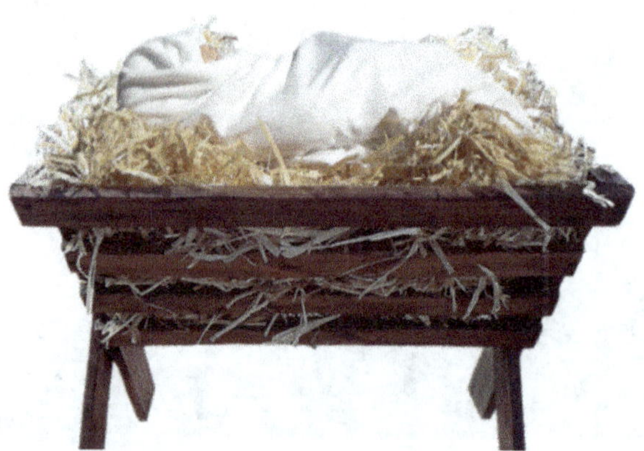

Pixabay: jeffjacobs1990.

**For unto you is born this day in the city of David
a Saviour, which is Christ the Lord.
And this shall be a sign unto you; Ye shall find the babe
wrapped in swaddling clothes, lying in a manger.**
~ Luke 2: 11-12

Art for All Ages

Draw a picture of a gift you like to give...

O give thanks to the LORD
for he is good:
for his mercy endureth for ever.
~ Psalm 107:1

Feet...

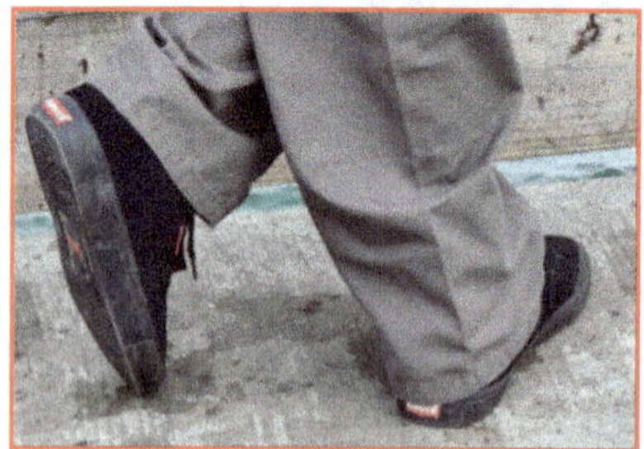

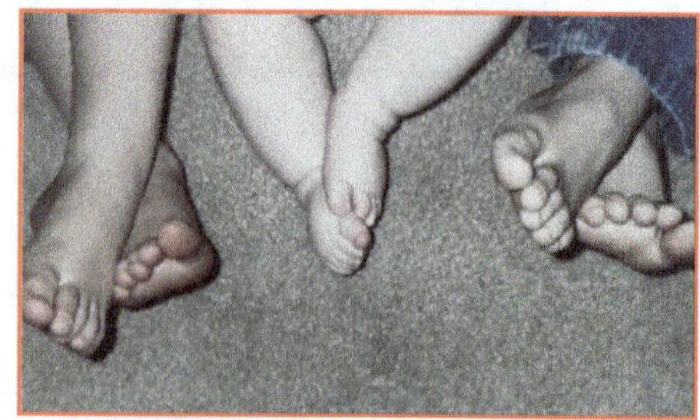

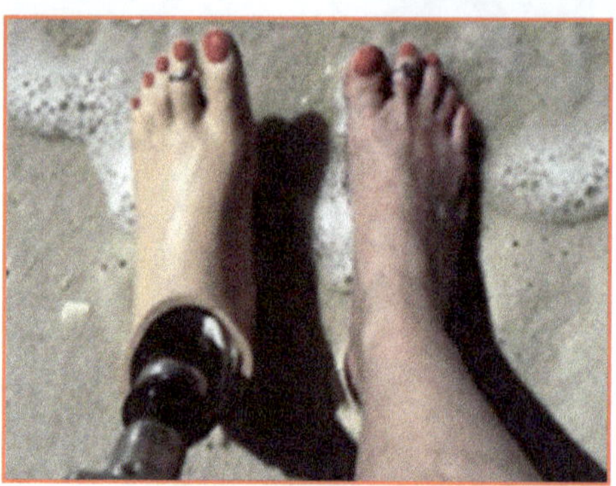

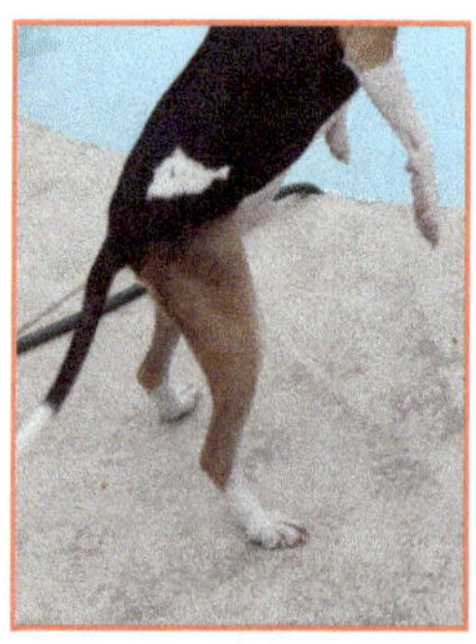

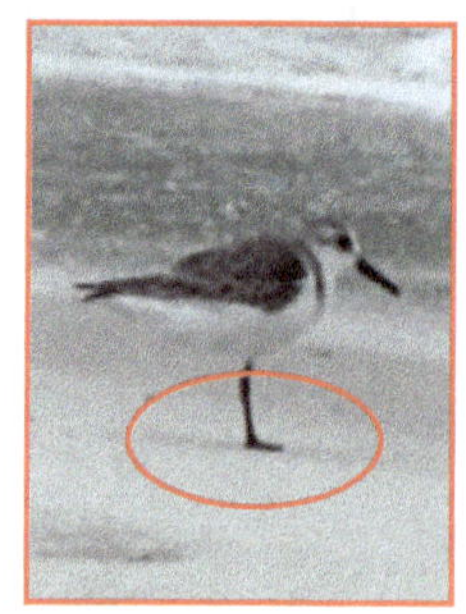

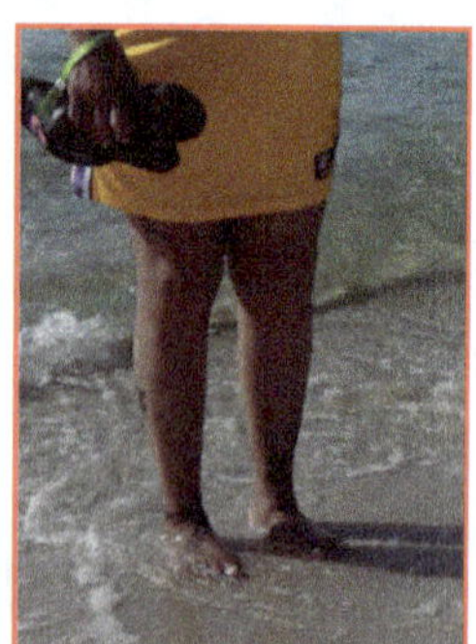

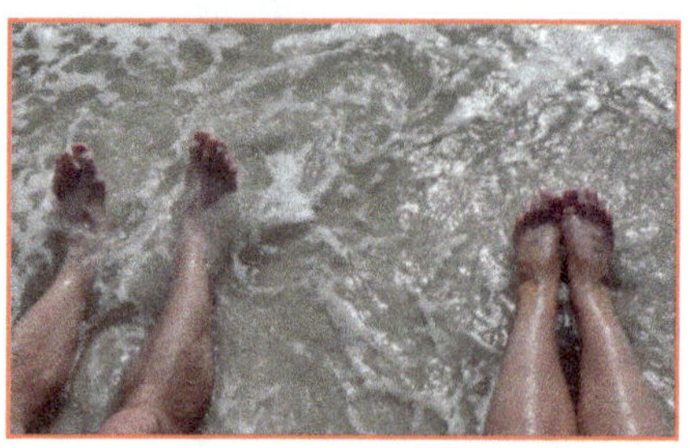

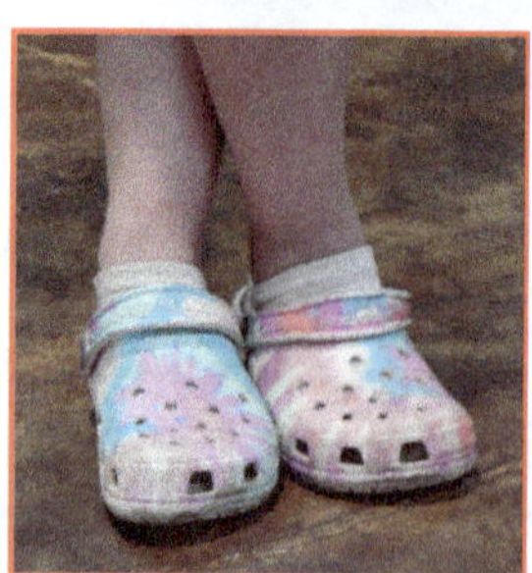

How beautiful are the feet
of them that preach the gospel of peace,
and bring glad tidings of good things!

~ Romans 13:10

Here I Am...
Linda Dwyer

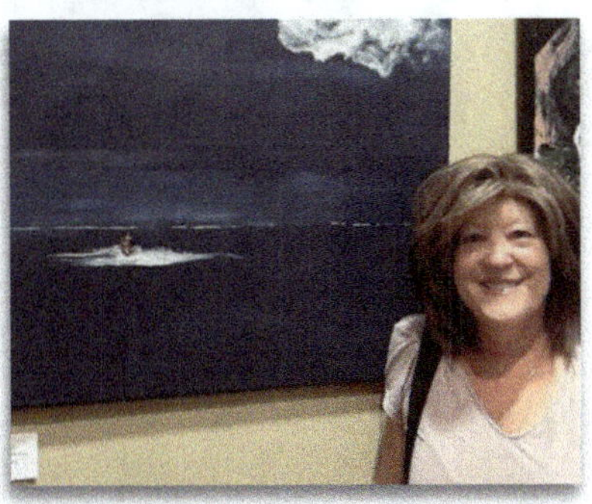

Here I am...

Linda Dwyer, a new friend, sister in the faith of Jesus, and an accomplished artist,* thought that six years ago. Nancy, her beloved mother-in-law had just died. Sean, Ryan, and Connor, her three sons, had left home and gone off to college...

Here I am...now what?

Linda wondered. For the past five years, Linda and Sean, her husband, had cared for Nancy. Prior to that time, Linda had focused on raising Sean, Ryan, and Connor, training them in the way they should go to become Godly men.

But now, Linda wondered, *Here I am... What now, Lord?*

On August 25, 2016, Dr. Clarice Fluitt, an evangelist, specifically prayed for Linda and her family. He asked God to open new doors for them; that they would be purpose and destiny filled. The next day Linda prayed, "God, what is my purpose for now? What do you want me to do?"

Linda said she immediately heard God speak to her heart, "I want you to paint."

In September, Linda found a paintbrush, several canvases, and a few tubes of leftover acrylic paint that Connor, her now graphic designer son, had left at home. That day, Linda began to paint. "I had never painted before, but I wanted to be obedient," Linda said, "so—I decided to start painting. In my heart, I knew that God had given me this precious gift for his glory." Linda's family encouraged her. Several weeks later, God opened the door for Joy Works Paintings.

From the "get-go," from that time and even today, although she had never thought about painting professionally, Linda felt a boldness and confidence she knew came from God. As she painted, mixing mini mountains of purple, blue, gold, green, and other hues of colors, Linda thought, *I'm having so much fun.* Since she first picked up Connor's paintbrush, Linda completed more than 1700 paintings. Some nights, she would paint as many as eight paintings.

Whenever she sits down to paint, Linda prays over the canvas, "Lord, will you please bless whoever sees or receives this painting with your joy and peace. Let them be drawn to Jesus." After Linda finishes each unique creation, posts a picture of it on social media.

In November 2016, during her first art show, Linda sold 60 paintings and received several commissions to paint even more.

"When I first began to paint," Linda admitted, "during a phone conversation, an artist friend asked me, 'What kind of media are you using?'"

"I use watercolor on canvas," Linda replied.

"Oh Linda... you don't use watercolor on canvas. You're supposed to use acrylic or oil paints," her friend said.

"I have to change the way I've been doing things... " she told her friend, "I can't believe I didn't know this. After taking lessons from M. Douglas Walton, an internationally renowned artist who lives in her hometown, Linda began to paint with Benjamin Moore house paints.

People also often ask or email Linda questions like, "How did you find your purpose? How do I find my purpose in life?"

God revealed His gift to Linda when she prayed and cried out to Him. She specifically prayed, "Lord, what do you want me to do to help others and glorify you? God not only gave her the precious gift of painting, He also placed an overpowering desire in her to use that gift. Today, Linda prays that when people see her work, they see Jesus; that they experience Him through her work.

"When I reflect on the time since September 2017," Linda said, "I am in awe. It would have been impossible for me to accomplish what I have done in painting on my own. "God makes the impossible possible" (Romans 15:1), she stresses. "He not only gave me the precious gift of painting, His strength, presence, and power work through me as I paint."

"Pray and cry out to God," Linda stresses. "Ask Him what He wants you to do. Be obedient and do what God calls you to do."

When God speaks to us, we also need to respond similar to the way Eli instructed Samuel when God called him. "Speak, Lord; for thy servant heareth" (1 Samuel 3:9b).

Linda listened and obeyed God when He answered her prayer and called her to paint to reflect His light, love, and life in Jesus. No matter the gift God gives us, nor whatever He calls us to do, we need to obey and do likewise. We need to say to God, "Here I am..."

www.joyworkspaintings.com

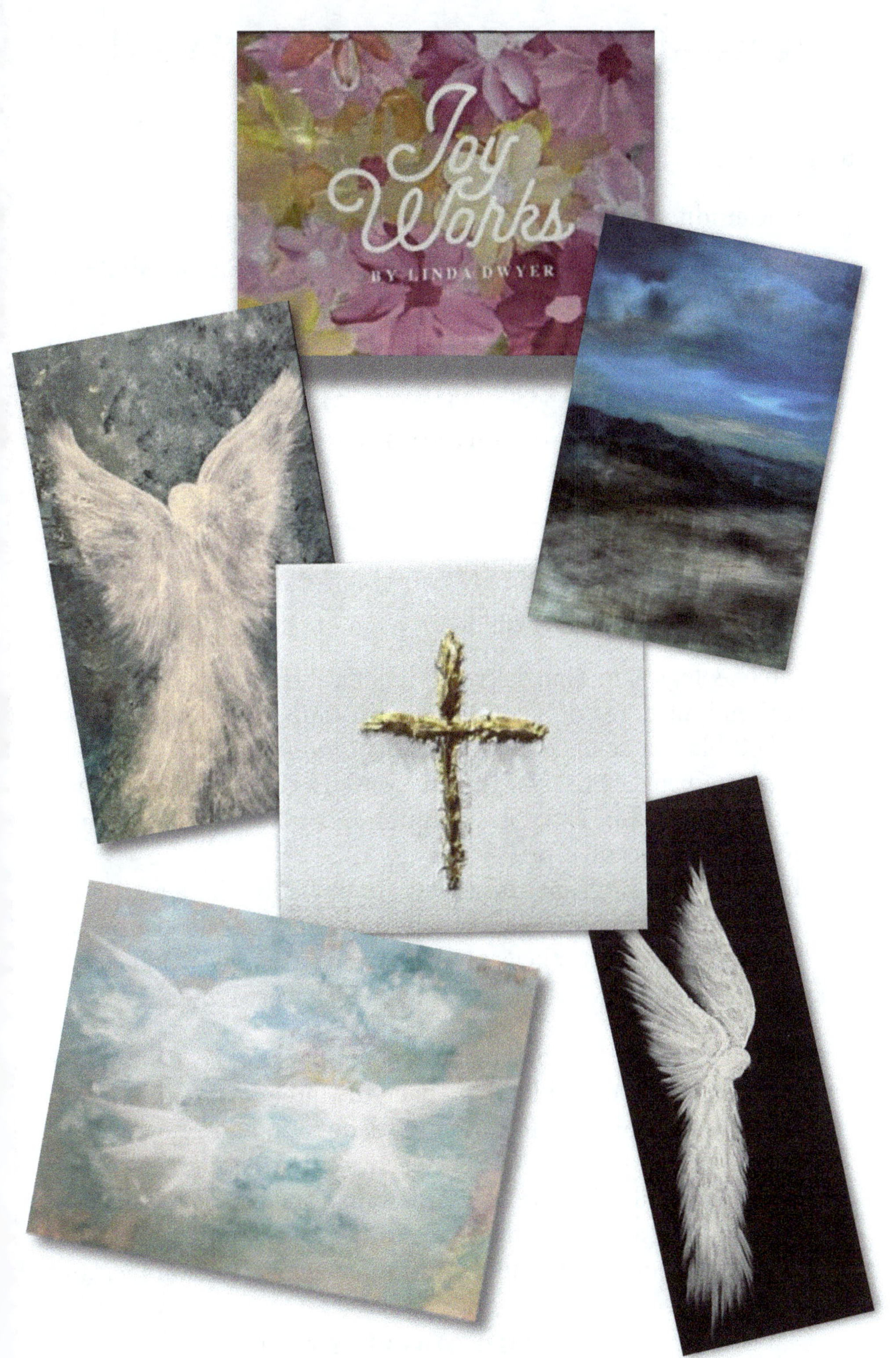

* www.joyworkspaintings.com

Words from and about "The Word"

Long before scientists confirmed the following facts of nature, the Bible recorded:

- ➢ Roundness of the earth **(Isaiah 40:22 -** page 12**)**
- ➢ Almost infinite extent of the sidereal universe **(Isaiah 55:9-** page 36**)**
- ➢ Law of conservation of mass and energy **(II Peter 3:7-** page 8**)**
- ➢ Hydrologic cycle **(Ecclesiastes 1:7-** page 10**)**
- ➢ Vast number of stars **(Jeremiah 33:22-** page 11**)**
- ➢ Law of increasing entropy **(Psalm 102:25-27-** page 15 **)**
- ➢ Importance of blood in life processes **(Leviticus 17:11-** page 16**)**
- ➢ Atmospheric circulation **(Ecclesiastes 1:6-** page - 17 **)**
- ➢ Gravitational field **(Job 26:7-** page - 18**)**

No archaeological finding discredits a biblical reference. IN the past, the National Academy of Sciences listed 100 discrepancies between the Holy Bible and science. Now, only *debatably* a few exist.

Isaiah predicted Christ's birthplace, as well as His death place, tand he way He would die. The book of Isaiah records how much money would be paid to betray Christ.

More than 40 different authors wrote the Holy Bible over 1,500 years at different times in history. Although enemies have attached this book more than any other, It has amazingly survived. In the book, *Evidence that Demands A Verdict,* Josh McDowell wrote:

From the days of the Roman emperors to present day communist countries, it [the Holy Bible] has been the target of complete anni-hilation and continues to thrive in readership and reference. (Amazing for a book that merely teaches submission to governing authorities, goodwill toward your fellow man and personal diligence). Not only do all authors agree on the same subject, unlike any other great work, they are painfully frank about their shortcomings and failures.

Every word of God is pure;
He is a shield to those who put their trust in Him.

~ Proverbs 30:5

Natchitoches Christmas Festival

In 2020, USA Today named Louisiana's Natchitoches Christmas Festival the "Best Public Holiday Light Display" [by 10 Best Readers' Choice]. This year, the 96th year old festival runs from November 19th, 2022 – January 6th, 2023, and features more than 100 lighted set pieces and 350,000 lights. Each evening at dusk during this season, Christmas lights illuminate downtown Natchitoches and Cane River Lake.

In addition to fireworks displays each Saturday, the festival features carriage tours through the National Historic Landmark District, and live entertainment. The Natchitoches Historic Foundation presents the Northwestern State University Christmas Gala, and the Christmas Tour of Homes.

Since 1927, Natchitoches (pronounced Nack-a-tish), named after a Native American tribe, the oldest permanent settlement in the Louisiana Purchase Territory, has served as home to one of the oldest community-based holiday celebrations in America. The Natchitoches Christmas Festival Starting began as a one-day festival, but evolved into a six-week long Christmas Season.

To get there, take exit #138 off of I-49.

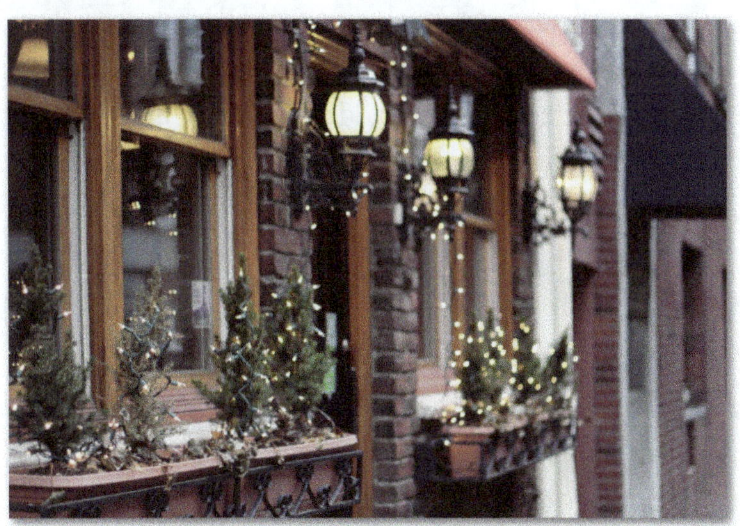

StockSnap from Pixabay

**Then spake Jesus again unto them,
saying, I am the light of the world:
he that followeth me shall not walk in darkness,
but shall have the light of life.**

Hot Chocolate Mix

2 cups nonfat dry milk powder   1 cup cocoa powder

2 cups confectioner's sugar   Dash of salt

1 cup powdered coffee creamer

- ➢ Mix all ingredients together well.
- ➢ Spoon into jars or mugs. Affix lid.

To Make Hot Chocolate:

To make 1 cup, fill a mug ¼ to ⅓ full of mix, stirring in 6 to 8 ounces of very hot water. Stir well. Add mini marshmallows if desired.

Linda's Personal Note:

When making this for gift giving, I put mix in a pint-sized Mason jar, leaving about two inches head space. Using the back of a spoon to pack the mix a little, I add a handful of mini semi-sweet chocolate chips and some mini marshmallows.

The mix recipe will make about 1 quart jar and ½ pint jar.

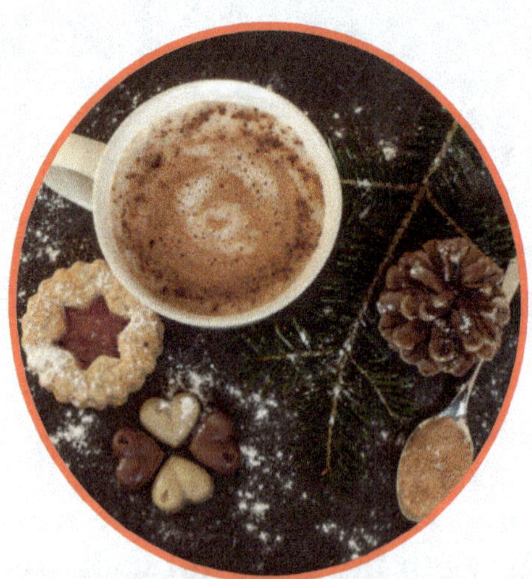

Pixabay: Sabrina Ripke

Southern Spiced Tea

2 jars (7 ounces each) Tang® orange-flavored drink mix
2½ cups sugar
2 teaspoons ground cloves
2 teaspoons powdered cinnamon
1 teaspoon nutmeg
⅔ cup instant iced tea mix
2 small (.23 ounce each) packages Wyler's® Lemonade mix

➢ Mix all ingredients together in bowl.

➢ For gift giving, put mix in pint sized jars, add some ribbon or twine, and attach the instructions.

To Make Spiced Tea:

Spoon 2½ to 3 heaping teaspoons into a cup and add very hot water. Stir until dissolved.

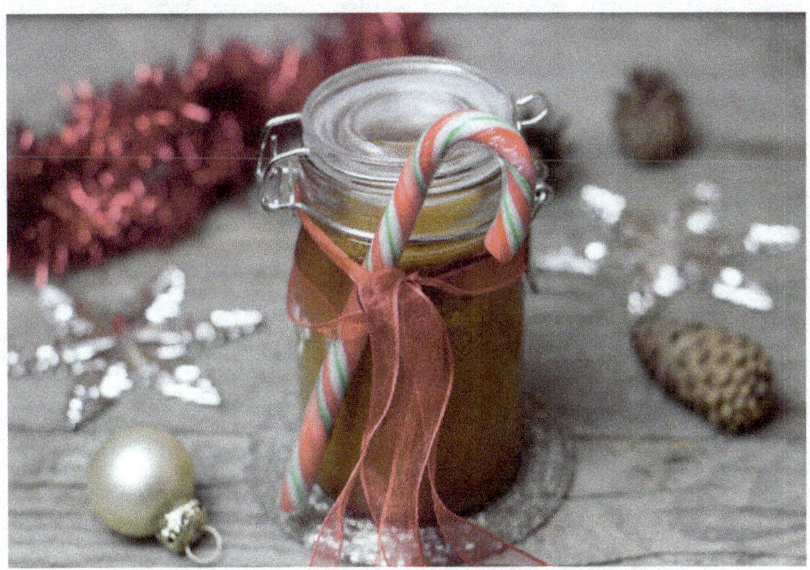

Bernadette Wurzinger from Pixabay

All-Purpose Quick Baking Mix

10 cups all-purpose flour (can use ½ whole wheat flour, if desired)
2 cups nonfat dry milk powder or buttermilk powder
6 tablespoons baking powder
1 tablespoon salt
½ tablespoon cream of tartar
2½ cups vegetable shortening

> ➢ In a large bowl, sift the dry ingredients together.

> ➢ With pastry blender (or two knives or your fingers), cut in shortening until mixture resembles cornmeal in texture.

> ➢ Store in airtight container. Use as needed.

Quick Biscuits:

> ➢ Preheat oven to 450°.

> ➢ Stir together 3 cups Quick Baking Mix and ¾ cup milk or water until blended.

> ➢ Drop by spoonfuls onto baking sheet.

> ➢ Bake for 10 to 12 minutes or until golden brown.

Linda's Personal Note:

Garlic Cheese Biscuits can be made using 2 cups quick mix, 1 cup shredded cheddar cheese and ⅔ cup milk. Mix and bake at 450° for 10 to 12 minutes. Melt ¼ cup butter and ¼ teaspoon garlic powder in microwave. Brush over hot biscuits.

All Purpose Quick Mix can be used in any recipe that calls for Bisquick™ or biscuit mix such as biscuits, pancakes, scones, coffee cake, sausage cheese balls, taco pie, and more.

Brownie Mix

8 cups sugar
6 cups unbleached all-purpose flour
2 cups cocoa powder
1½ tablespoons baking powder
1 tablespoon salt

> ➤ Mix ingredients together until well blended.

> ➤ Store in airtight container.

To Make Brownies:

¼ cup brownie mix
2 eggs, beaten
⅓ cup canola oil (or melted butter)
2 teaspoons vanilla
½ cup chopped nuts or chocolate chips (optional)

> ➤ Preheat oven to 350°. Grease an 8 x 8-inch square pan.

> ➤ Combine ingredients and mix until smooth.

> ➤ Bake for 30 to 35 minutes until center is firm.

> ➤ Cool.

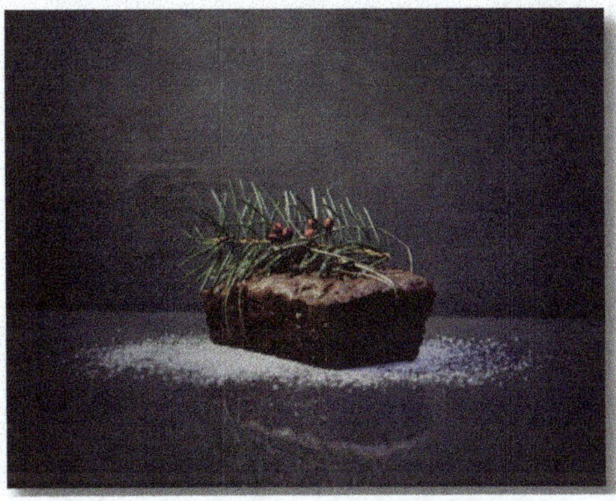

Pixabay: Jill Heyer

Texas Sheet Cake

4 cups brownie mix
½ cup oil
1 cup water
½ cup sour cream
2 eggs, slightly beaten
1 teaspoon vanilla
1 teaspoon baking soda

➤ Preheat oven to 375°.
  Grease a 15 x 10-inch jelly roll pan or sheet cake pan.

➤ Put brownie mix in bowl.
  In saucepan, bring oil, water and sour cream to a boil.
  Add to the brownie mix.

➤ Stir in eggs, vanilla and baking soda. Pour into pan.

➤ Bake 20 to 25 minutes or until toothpick inserted in center comes out clean.

➤ Prepare frosting while cake is baking and frost while cake is hot.

Frosting:

½ cup evaporated milk
½ cup butter
¼ cup cocoa powder
3 cups powdered sugar
2 teaspoons vanilla

➤ Bring milk, butter and cocoa powder to a boil in saucepan. Remove from heat. Add powdered sugar and vanilla. Stir until smooth.

➤ Immediately spread over cake after removing from oven.

➤ Allow cake to cool before cutting and serving.

Almond Coconut Balls

Lahcen Belkimite

Ingredients

4 large eggs
1 cup granulated raw or white sugar
2 cups almond flour
2 cups unsweetened shredded coconut
1 ½ cups sweetened coconut
1 teaspoon vanilla extract
1 teaspoon almond extracts
1 teaspoon baking powder
⅛ teaspoon salt
Powdered sugar for coating dough balls
Orange blossom water
Miniature muffin cups

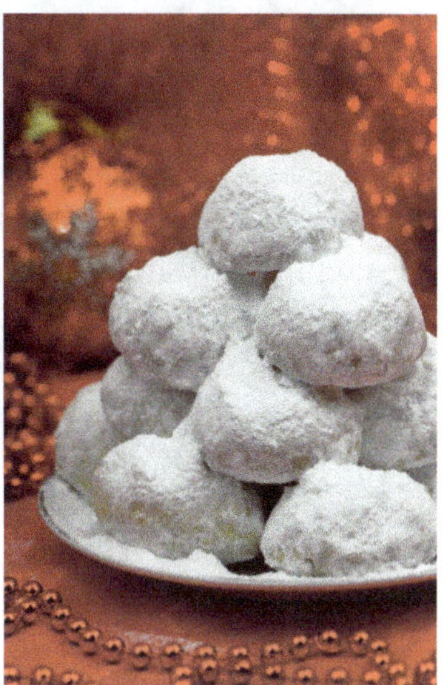

Directions

Preheat over to 355°.

Crack eggs and whisk until blended. Gradually add sugar, and beat slowly until foamy. Add vanilla and almond extracts and blend into egg/sugar mixture.

In separate bowl, mix almond flour, baking powder, and salt. Add this mixture with egg/sugar blend. Fold in coconut. Use hands to mix thoroughly.

Using melon scoop, to form small balls of dough. Dampen fingers with orange blossom water. Gently roll balls into powdered sugar to lightly coat.

Position muffin cups on baking sheets and place one pastry ball into each. Bake until the tops of coconut almond balls crack; approximately for 15 minutes.

How sweet are thy words unto my taste!
yea, sweeter than honey to my mouth!
~ Psalm 119:103

Five Vital "How to..." Survival Skills*

1. How to start and sustain a fire...

Fire enables you to cook your food, stay warm and help scare away any wild varmints that might be on the prowl. To start a fire, you need a "firestarter" such as waterproof matches or slivers of wood, or small twigs as well as dry leaves, or pine needles work to help bring flames to life.

2. How to construct a short-term survival shelter...

A temporary shelter shields you from the elements. Securing available resources depends on your weather, climate, and terrain. To help you retain your body heat in cold weather as well as protect yourself from the sun and stay hydrated in hot weather, you need to insulate the shelter you create.

3. How to prioritize your priorities...

According to the subjective "rule of threes," the average human can survive:
- three hours without shelter,
- three days without water, and
- three weeks without food.

The threes offer a guide for actions in a serious survival situation.

4. How to find a clean water source...

In a survival scenario, finding and collecting drinking water proves critical. You should either use a fire to boil water, or a water filter or iodine tablets to purify it. Stay hydrated.

5. How to locate and secure food...

Forage your surrounding area for edible flowers, roots, and nuts. Build snares from natural materials to trap small game, or fabricate fishing tools to catch fish. Gather extra food when possible. Diversify your diet for essential protein, fats, vitamins, and minerals.

*www.masterclass.com/articles/survival-tips#1tbhAZL1PmnzzsPRLz3rlG

Every moving thing that liveth shall be meat for you; even as the green herb have I given you all things.

~ Genesis 9:3

A Night of No Slumber
Clint Clarneau

T'was a night of no slumber,
With stars shining bright.
We talked as we kept watch
Of our sheep flocks by night.

The night, as it fell
Seemed like any other,
But something before dawn
Would change us forever.

The twinkling stars glittered.
For my eyes, such a feast,
But one shone much brighter,
Just off to the east.

We knew, as we'd taught
True stories of old,
But this night would bring us
The best ever told...

From up on the hillsides,
This dark, dank night,
We could see in the distance
Bethlehem's light.

Then out of night sky
In a series of blazes,
Thousands of angels sang,
Proclaiming God's praises

Not one shepherd moved
Or dared even try,
As we stared with great awe,
At this Heavenly Sight.

"Peace on Earth," angels sang,
"And good will to all men."
Nine thousand? we wondered,
No...must be more than ten.

Just as the angel told us,
We nodded and smiled.
Wrapped snugly with love,
Before us—the Christ Child.

Yet there we were standing,
With God's Only Son.
Of all nights in my life,
I most treasure this one.

Some believed; others wondered
About things seen and heard,
'Our story's true, we tell them,
'Recorded in God's Holy Word.

While some would accept,
And others refuse,
We never stopped sharing
God's gift—the Good News.

Christ came to renew lives
That sin had revoked.
'Twas a night of no slumber,
Yet—a night full of hope.

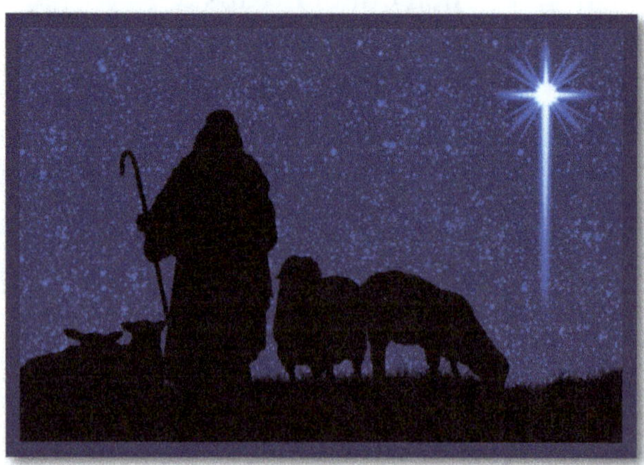

Christmas Card Citations
Verses

I [Jesus] have told you these things,
so that in me you may have peace.
In this world you will have trouble.
But take heart! I have overcome the world.
~ John 16:33

But the angel said to them,
"Do not be afraid. I bring you good
news that will cause great joy for all the people.
~ Luke 2:10

Today in the town of David
a Savior has been born to you;
he is the Messiah, the Lord.
~ Luke 2:11

Worth Sharing

Once in our world, a stable had
something in it that was bigger than our whole world.

The Son of God became a man
to enable men
to become sons of God.
~ C.S. Lewis

**Who can add to Christmas?
The perfect motive is that
God so loved the world.
The perfect gift is that
He gave His only Son.
The only requirement is to
believe in Him.
The reward of faith is that
you shall have everlasting life.**
~ Corrie Ten Boom

The Gift of Changing Crappy Unhealthy Habits
Dr. Scott Jutte
(Excerpt from forthcoming book, *Better Health, Simple as THAT*)

Seventy thousand miles ago, due to me me being stupid," and driving too fast around a curve, I had to remind myself: *Instead of "being stupid," staying miserable, complaining about crappy health, why not change crappy health habits into healthy actions?*

Surviving a major motorcycle crash, my body hurt inside and out. The accident broke my collarbone. It fractured my lower back in two places.

For two days after my "being stupid" consequences, I took the medica-ation exactly as the ER doctor pre-

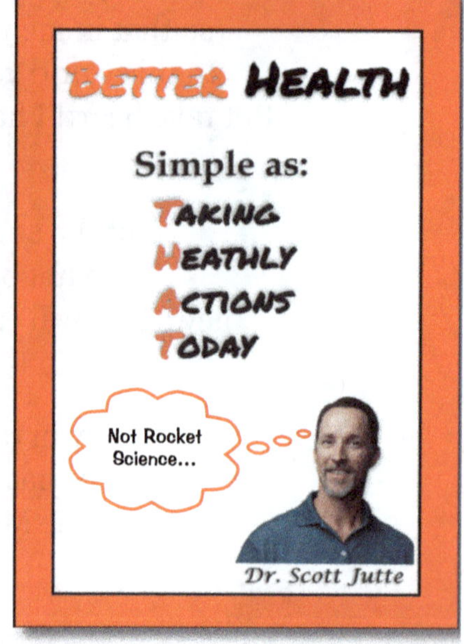

scribed. But then, I felt lethargic and miserable from the side effects of the medicine. I decided to stop taking the drugs… to change my treatment. I determined to experience natural pain relief and healing; to "tough out" the pain while my body healed.

I threw all the pain pills away. Within six weeks after my motorcycle crash, I returned to work full-time. Part of my personally prescribed "medicine" to help my body heal naturally included exercise.

People who do stupid things like driving a motorcycle too fast around a curve don't have the right to complain about what happens as a result. People who don't take care of their bodies or their cars don't have a legitimate reason to complain when either of them fails to perform efficiently. People who don't exercise should not complain about health problems that evolve from the lack of exercise or eating an unhealthy diet.

Health, our most valuable physical possession, requires concen-trated care. Some people might say, "My family is my most valuable possession." If you do not have your health, I remind them, you cannot enjoy time with your family as much as when you are healthy. The presence and/or absence of health affects all aspects of, as well as our quality of life.

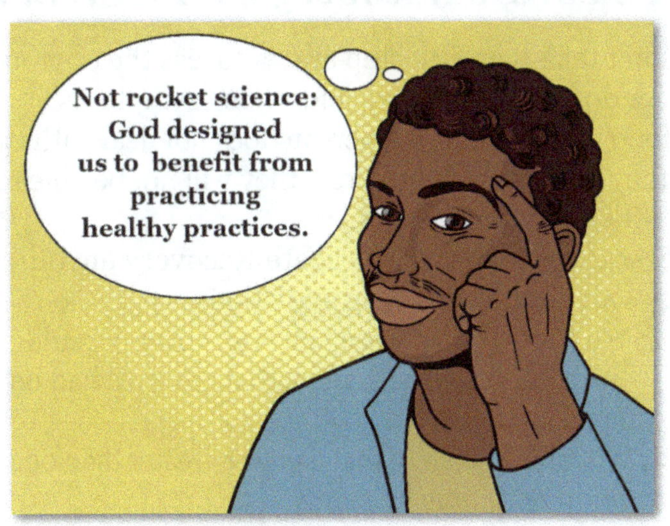

**Instead of complaining
about crappy health,
why not change
your crappy unhealthy habits
into healthy actions?**

**Why not
give yourself
the gift of better health?**

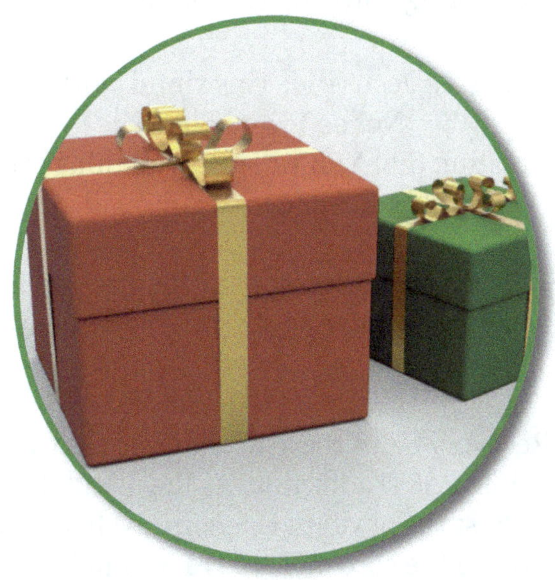

Celebrate Recovery's First Step...

"If you don't take that first step and address the obvious, how in the thunder do you address the underlying symptoms?"

Raymond stressed that if a person does not deal with the alcohol or drugs they know to be a problem, they will not be able to uncover and deal with underlying issues.

The first three steps in Celebrate Recovery encourage those struggling with alcohol and drug addiction:

Step 1: We admitted we were powerless over our addictions and compulsive behaviors, that our lives had become unmanageable.

Step 2: We came to believe that a power greater than ourselves could restore us to sanity.

Step 3: We made a decision to turn our wills and our lives over to the care of God.

The following relates the full original copy of the Serenity Prayer, also used in recovery groups (abbreviated format), that Reinhold Niebuhr (1892-1971) wrote.

God, give us grace to accept with serenity
the things that cannot be changed,
Courage to change the things which should be changed,
and the Wisdom to distinguish the one from the other.
Living one day at a time, enjoying one moment at a time,
Accepting hardship as a pathway to peace,

Taking, as Jesus did, This sinful world as it is,
Not as I would have it,
Trusting that You will make all things right,
If I surrender to Your will.

So that I may be reasonably happy in this life,
And supremely happy with You forever in the next.
Amen

Celebrate Recovery helps those dealing with as well as those who care for those battling A&D addiction, As Raymond stressed, take that first step and address the obvious. Get help... When we turn our wills and our lives over to the care of God, He will make all things right.

December 2022

Mon	Tue	Wed	Thu	Fri	Sat	Sun
			1	2	3	4
5	6	7	8	9	10	11
12	13	14	15	16	17	18
19	20	21	22	23	24	25
26	27	28	29	30	31	

One Road to Heaven; Many Roads to Hell

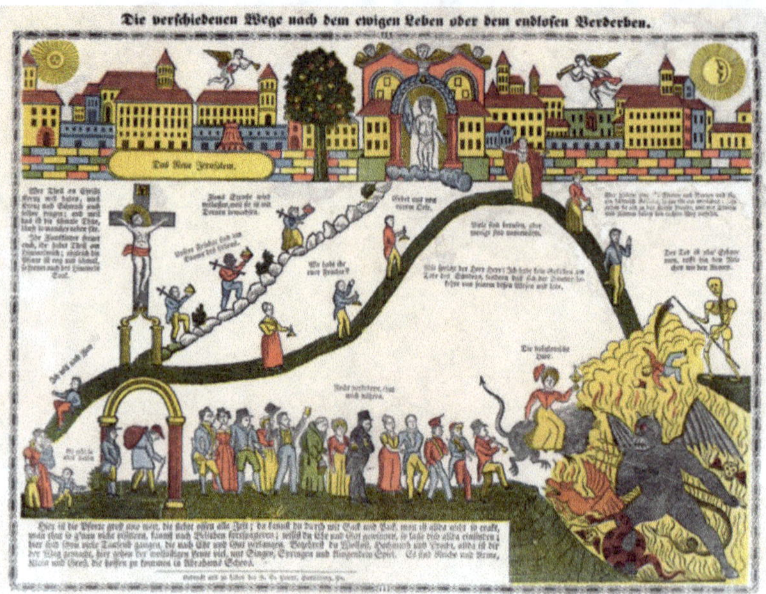

The Library Company of Philadelphia .

Lord Jesus,

I know all have sinned, and that includes me. I ask You to forgive me, come into my heart, and save me.

I receive Your gift of eternal life. I know You died for me, and shed Your blood as a sacrifice for my sins on the cross.

I know now that I am saved, born again, and going to Heaven because of You, Jesus.

I believe with my heart, and confess with my mouth that Jesus Christ is my Lord and Personal Savior.

~ Amen.

Your name: ________________________________

Date: __________ / __________ / __________

Time: _____:_____

John B. Vennell, PhD.
Faith Community South Church
3115 Main Street
Cottondale FL 32431

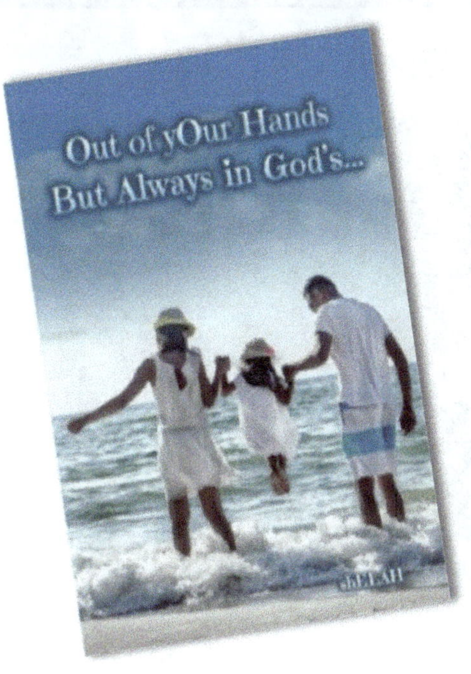

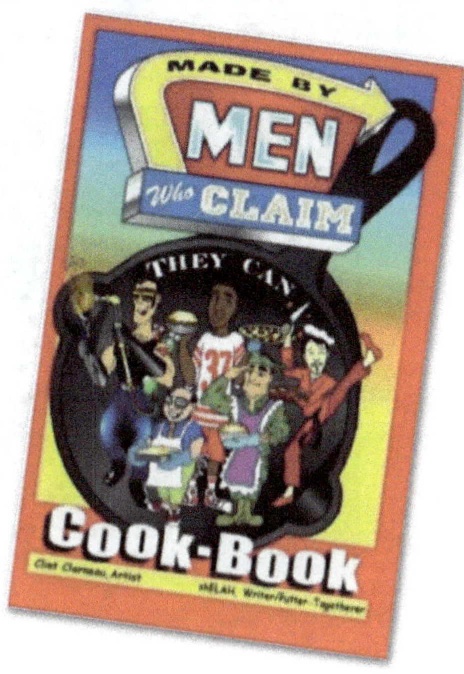

Books by yOur Backyard Publishing

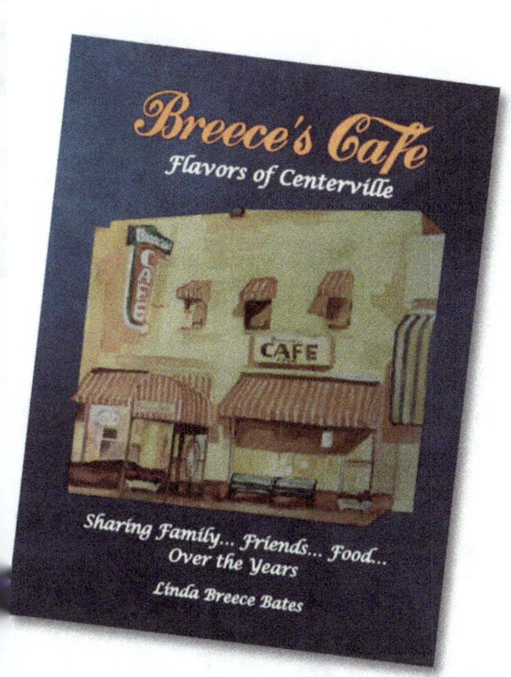

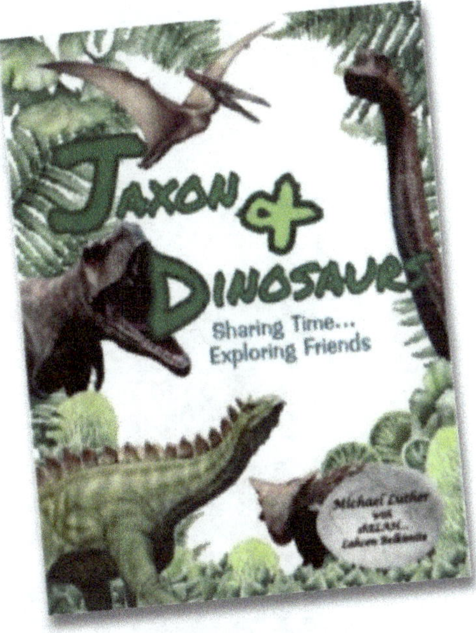

Sponsoring Opportunities

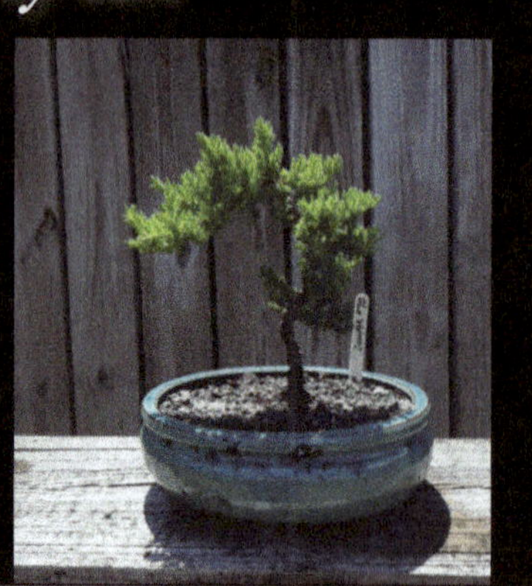

Bonsai by dori

3089 Marin St.
Cottondale, FL 32431

bonsaibydori.com
facebook.com/bonsaibydori

Open 7 Days

"Your Basic
Mom and Pop Bonsai Shop"

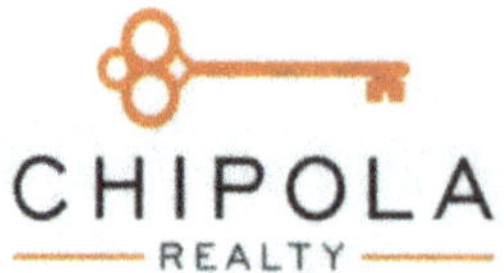

Office: (850) 482-4446
Fax: (850) 482-1009
rentals@chipola.com
www.chipola.com

4325 B Lafayette St
Marianna, FL 32446

Shirley Lowe & Susie Stevens

Property Management Department

after hours emergency # (850) 482-4446

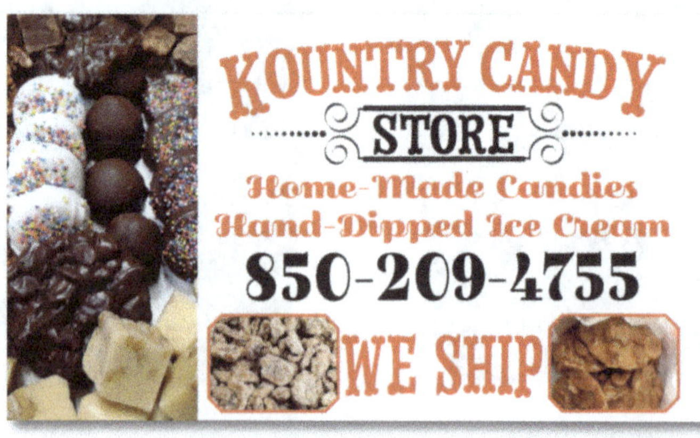

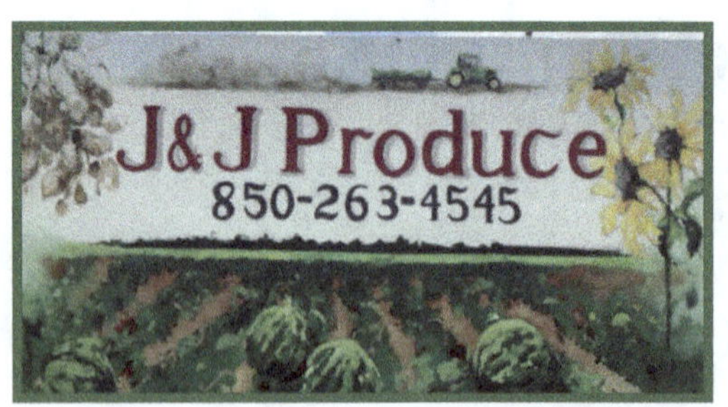

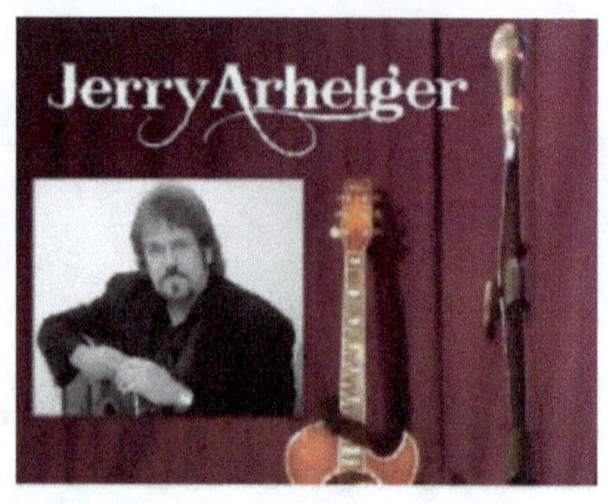

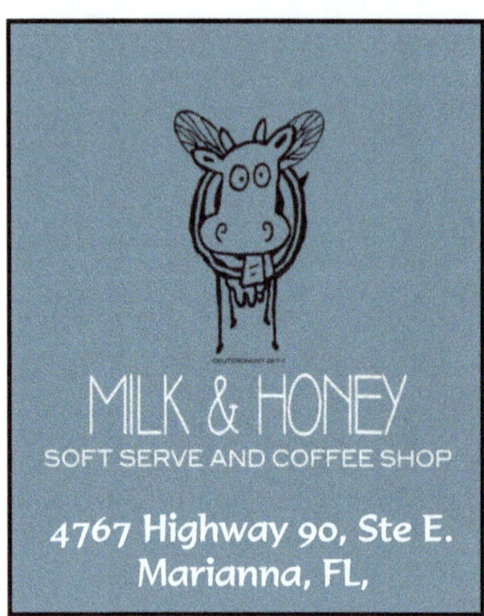

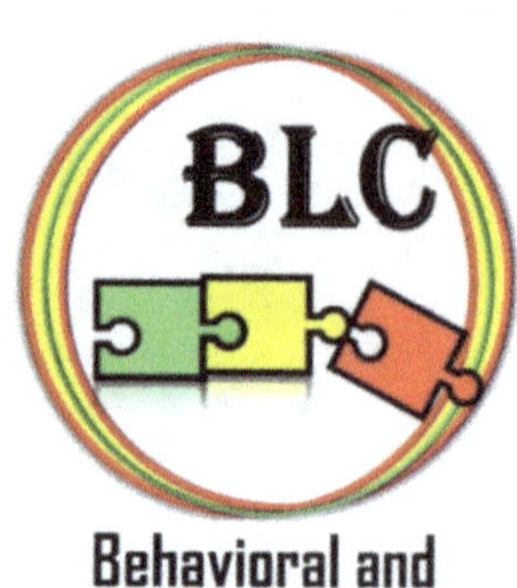

Windham Shoe Shop

Quality Shoe Repair & Western Shop

Double H ◆ Justin ◆ Dan Post ◆ Chippewa

{
Mon - Wed - Fri - 8:00 am to 5:00 pm
Tues - 8:00 am to 4:00 pm
Sat - 8:00 to 12 Noon
Closed Thursday & Sunday
}

BOOT & SHOE REPAIR

4408 LaFayette St.
Marianna, FL 32446

Dennis Creamer

(850)482-4227

Christmas...

And it came to pass in those days,
that there went out a decree from Caesar Augustus
that all the world should be taxed...

4 And Joseph also went up from Galilee, out of the city of Nazareth,
into Judaea, unto the city of David, which is called Bethlehem;
(because he was of the house and lineage of David:)

5 To be taxed with Mary his espoused wife,
being great with child.

6 And so it was, that, while they were there,
the days were accomplished that she should be delivered.

7 And she brought forth her firstborn son,
and wrapped him in swaddling clothes,
and laid him in a manger;
because there was no room for them in the inn.

8 And there were in the same country
shepherds abiding in the field,
keeping watch over their flock by night.

9 And, lo, the angel of the Lord came upon them,
and the glory of the Lord shone round about them:
and they were sore afraid.

10 And the angel said unto them, Fear not:
for, behold, I bring you good tidings of great joy,
which shall be to all people.

11 For unto you is born this day in the city of David
a Saviour, which is Christ the Lord.

12 And this shall be a sign unto you;
Ye shall find the babe wrapped in swaddling clothes,
lying in a manger.

13 And suddenly there was with the angel
a multitude of the heavenly host
praising God, and saying,

14 Glory to God in the highest,
and on earth peace, good will toward men.
~ Luke 2

Remember...

www.ingramcontent.com/pod-product-compliance
Lightning Source LLC
Chambersburg PA
CBHW050628070726
47592CB00029B/2865